Keeping Score

A Guide to Love and Relationships

Marc Brackett

Treinta y Tres Publishing
Twin Falls, Idaho
www.keepingscorebook.com

Keeping Score
A Guide to Love and Relationships

Copyright ©2011 by Marc Brackett

Marc Brackett
Treinta y Tres Publishing
Twin Falls, Idaho 2011
www.keepingscorebook.com

Cover design and inside layout: TheBookProducer.com
Fountain pen image courtsey of Waterman: www.waterman.com

Printed in the United States

Keeping Score: A Guide to Love and Relationships
ISBN 978-0-9834888-0-4

Acknowledgments

There are far too many people who have made this book a reality for me to individually mention them all. These individuals were willing to share aspects of their lives that have directly shaped the content of this book, thank you.

There also have been several people who through their editing (and willingness to continue reading) have made this book a readable product. My thanks to an exceptional mother-in-law, Elizabeth Mendenhall. I additionally want to thank Stephanie Lambert. Their editing skills and occasional criticism have been a fundamental part of finishing this book.

To my friend Tim, may the Lomo Slayer roll ever on.

I especially want to thank the love of my life, Kristin Brackett. She has not only helped write and edit this book, but has been an unyielding advocate of me getting things right! I have consistently been over my head in writing this book and would have never gotten this far without her support.

TABLE OF CONTENTS

PREFACE

All good things have a source of inspiration and often that source comes from an unlikely place. This book originated in a town called Treinta y Tres in the South American country of Uruguay, located between Brazil and Argentina.

Tim, a long time friend, and I were investigating real estate values in South America. After a morning spent walking through fields of rice, soybeans, and corn, we returned to Treinta y Tres for a late lunch. Out of the afternoon sun, in a small café off of the main plaza, we kicked back and enjoyed a meal. Time has a way of standing still in a Spanish speaking country, especially on a hot summer day while conversing with a best friend. For reasons we still don't quite understand, we started to talk about relationships.

We have had some very different experiences in our lives when it comes to relationships. Recently, Tim had the pleasure of attending his ex-wife's wedding while accompanying their two small children. There were the curious glances from the other guests and the awkward moment of watching the woman he had loved repeat the same words he had once heard to another man. This event really brought home the magnitude of the marriage's failure and the impact it was going to continue having on his life.

The years of an unhealthy relationship, the dissolution of the marriage, the stress of raising children without a partner, and the never ending conflict that divorce brings about, are engraved in Tim's face. Not only had the entire tragedy aged him considerably, but it had worn him out mentally, physically, and spiritually. There are things in life that cannot be undone or forgotten and just have to be lived with. When a relationship ends, the reality is that personal connections are often too deep to completely sever, particularly when children are involved. Relationships are supposed to be enjoyable and make life better. Tim's failed marriage had brought complete destruction and never ending chaos to his life.

Why did his marriage fail? Was there something wrong with him, was his ex-wife the problem, or were the two just a poor match? What actions sealed the fate of this union? Perhaps more importantly, had he learned anything from the failure of this relationship that would lessen the probability of future relationships ending the same way?

With these questions in mind, I had to look at my own marriage. My story is a bit different from Tim's. While I wish that I could claim superior intelligence or luck, divine assistance is the only phrase to appropriately describe how I landed the relationship with my wife. I've been married for almost sixteen years to a beautiful and intriguing woman named Kristin. She has blessed me with five equally beautiful daughters, all of whom continue to shape my world more than anything else I have ever been exposed to.

In all honesty, neither one of us can say our relationship has always been easy or enjoyable. We have had our share of trials and tribulations, but still my wife and I have managed to make it to this point. How did we get this far? What actions can we take to sustain our relationship into the future?

As the afternoon wore on, Tim and I tried to put the pieces together by examining Tim's failed marriage for fatal flaws. Just as after a jet crashes, the wreckage is reassembled and the flight plan is reviewed. We also looked at my still intact marriage to see why it was still flying (in spite of an extended South American walkabout). To our surprise, the two relationships didn't appear substantially different on the surface. Was it just one extreme event that had put Tim's life into shambles, was it faulty maintenance, or was his relationship a plane that never should have left the hangar?

The pieces began to fall into place once we expanded our examination to our friends' marriages and other relationships from our pasts. Persistent patterns began to appear, too frequent to be chance. We were able to identify reliable indicators of a relationship's failure or success. The question then became, how do we make sense of it all? We had found what to measure and now needed to determine how to measure it.

As evening approached, we worked on creating a mathematical point system to score relationships. Throughout the following weeks, we continued to expand and refine our relationship scoring model. Once home in the United States, I spent the next six months reading every piece of scientific literature on relationships I could find. The science validated what had started as common sense observations. After a few modifications I started field testing the relationship model on friends and other people I might encounter. The goal was to make sure the score reflected how people actually felt about their relationships. This period was enlightening as it showed where the points needed to be adjusted and identified factors that had been overlooked. My South American trip did not lead to any real estate ventures, but instead led to the creation of a common sense guide to relationship evaluation called *Keeping Score*.

Relationships are supposed to be fun and a source of positive value in your life. In our world today, we witness far too many relationships depriving people of the joy a relationship should provide. Whether you are single and trying to see if a relationship has the qualities it needs to fly, or married and needing to perform some in-flight maintenance, I believe this book will provide you with answers. Additionally, I hope you have as much fun using *Keeping Score* as I had creating it. Life is supposed to be fun and a healthy relationship can make life that much more enjoyable.

Keeping Score

INTRODUCTION

*K*eeping Score is a common sense approach to relationship evaluation intertwined with grade school math. Have you ever wondered how it is possible to launch rockets from Earth and have them land on Mars exactly on time years later? It really *is* rocket science. One must know the variables, plan extensively, and do the mathematical calculations. Rockets are not launched using hunches or feelings.

In relationships people often use only feelings to guide them and hope against their better judgment that the relationship will work. This approach may work well for some, but in today's world one would do better to stack the odds in their favor. Consider the following facts: around 50% of all first marriages end in divorce, 67% of second marriages end in divorce, and 74% of third marriages end in divorce (Divorce Peers). It would appear that even practice doesn't improve the odds of success. If we can send rockets across millions of miles of space with regular success, surely we can do better with something we can reach out and touch.

Let's start with what every relationship needs and define it, love. For starters, love is something you <u>can</u> feel for other people. "Can" is the key word here, as love is not something you <u>must</u> feel for other people.

Love is a personal choice, so how is it you decide to love someone? Think of the things you love. Love is a response to a positive experience, sensation, or interaction. Love is directly linked with joy. There is no way you will ever love getting a parking ticket or the sound of a dentist's drill, even though both are a necessary part of life. You love someone because of how they make you feel. A relationship is a collection of experiences, sensations, and interactions between two people that are both positive and negative. How you feel about someone is directly influenced by the balance of positive to negative. I have chosen to call these positives and negatives, <u>factors</u>, as their values can change.

To properly evaluate a relationship you first need to know what factors are important and what the significance of these factors are. While many of the same factors are important to both women and men, the significance of these factors in a relationship can be quite different. The order of significance is determined by biological and cultural influences. A number of factors that appear to be identical are experienced very differently by each gender.

Keeping Score has four components. The first component of *Keeping Score*, "Adam and Eve," is an evaluation divided into four sections for each gender. Three of the sections are unique for each sex with only a few factors being similar. The fourth section is identical for both partners. By reading the information offered prior to a factor, you will have a better understanding of how the factor should be interpreted. Also, be sure to correctly identify your status (single, married) when the set of factors is presented. Record your answers on the evaluation forms provided at the back of the book (pages 109-116) and continue until you have completed the evaluation. After completing the evaluation you will utilize the key (pages 104-107) to determine the relationship score.

The second component of *Keeping Score*, "Knowledge is Power," provides insight into the factors creating the relationship score. The factors are explained in greater detail with suggestions that may improve the score and ultimately the relationship.

The third component of *Keeping Score*, "A Score to Win," explains how to utilize your relationship score and then apply your own common sense to move towards the relationship you desire. The evaluation, coupled with the summary, will provide a clear and concise assessment of the relationship's current condition relative to the strengths and weaknesses of the partners.

The fourth component of *Keeping Score* is found at the website **www. keepingscorebook.com**. Here you can see how your relationship compares to other relationships. You can also share comments and see how other couples have addressed different factors. While every relationship has its own unique set of issues, there is a substantial amount we can learn from each other. In addition, for those interested, the factors will be discussed in greater detail with supporting scientific documentation provided.

Ladies first, please turn to page 5 and begin. Men can begin on page 53.

PART I

Eve

Let me start by saying, "Thank you." Odds are you were the person who purchased this book and I sincerely hope it will make a difference in your life. At times, it is important to evaluate the role we play in our lives and in the lives of others. In this component you will begin this process of evaluation, taking steps towards finding answers and accountability. Make no mistake here, this book will not mention "protective cocoons" or how to find the "inner you," but rather provide you with the tools to make an honest evaluation of your relationship. Whether you are single, trying to determine the marriage potential of a partner, or married, wanting to see how your relationship may be improved, the following pages will give you some direction.

> ➤ Use the relationship evaluation forms on
>   pages 109-112 to record your answers. Refer
>   to page 108 for an example of how to use the
>   evaluation forms.

Big Sword vs. Broken Sword

This section is about the ability of your partner to provide financially. Money is the sword of this time and place. There is a reason why the fairy tales we read growing up never mentioned the fierce accountant with his tax returns. Back when these tales were written a man needed a strong arm, sharp sword, and gold. Today we need brains, clever lawyers, and more gold yet. Money buys a home in a better neighborhood, family vacations, and cars with enhanced safety features. Even if you have your own sword that's bigger, sharper, and shinier, there is still value in having another big sword within sleeping distance. Who knows what dragon may show up in your driveway?

* * * * *

CASTLE OR CAVE

When it comes to money it doesn't hurt to have a head start. Whether your partner has had financial success or is still panning for gold, in the race for money it matters. Even more important, does your partner have destructive habits depleting current funds or preventing him from finding the gold? You instinctively know the answers to the following questions; hesitation on your part indicates you don't like the answer.

1. Does he have money?

    a. Yes

    b. No

2. Does your partner have any issues with gambling, alcohol, or other substance abuse problems?

    a. No

    b. There are some concerns

    c. Yes

King or Squire

Most women desire to marry someone with an equal or greater financial potential than their own. There's no fairy tale about the princess who settles for the inn keeper's drunken son, or at least there's no happily ever after ending to such a story. A prince may not be available, but the princess always finds a charming young lad whose talents and personality will take him to the top. This segment evaluates the "King in Training" and his chances of making it to the throne.

3.　**Education level of your partner**

    a.　No high school diploma

    b.　High school diploma or equivalent

    c.　Some college

    d.　College degree, certified trade (electrician, plumber, etc…)

    e.　Masters degree, PHD

4. **Work ethic of your partner**

    a. Driven, inventor of the "working vacation"

    b. Motivated, member of the "Thank God it's Monday Club"

    c. Productive, gets the job done and makes the world go round

    d. Clock watcher, never misses a break

    e. Air consumer, watching them work is more work than the task they are performing

5. **How many of the following behaviors or attitudes do you see in your partners interactions with others?**

| **Arrogance** | **Self-centeredness** | **Contempt** |
| **Negativity** | **Offensive remarks** | **Belittling** |

    a. None of the behaviors/attitudes are present

    b. Less than half of the behaviors/attitudes are present

    c. Half of the behaviors/attitudes are present

    d. More than half of the behaviors/attitudes are present

....

"Attitude is a little thing that makes a big difference."
~ Winston Churchill

....

INCOME BALANCE

This segment explores how income is distributed between partners, their earning capacity, and the ever elusive balance between work and relationships. As money is related to power, and control usually comes with power, it is very important to keep a balance. A review of the factors is required to see what the issues may be.

6. **Income distribution of earnings**

    a.   Your partner makes more money

    b.   You both have comparable incomes

    c.   You make more money than your partner

7. **Is your partner's life balanced in proportion to work?**

    a.   Yes

    b.   No

8. Does your partner have the capability to make an equitable contribution to the relationship? Include aspects other than financial as well.

   a.   Yes
   b.   No

Factor relating to Income Balance for _single_ women only

9. Have you discussed financial matters with your partner and come to a workable arrangement?

   a.   Yes, he's going to do what I tell him to
   b.   No, the lawyers can sort it out later

Factor relating to Income Balance for _married_ women only

9. How well is the financial understanding between you and your partner working (bank accounts, credit cards, big item purchases, retirement planning, etc)?

   a.   It's almost as smooth as no money down and twelve easy payments
   b.   Something is wrong here

Tried & True

This section is about factors related to making a woman feel loved. How well your partner demonstrates he loves, honors, and cherishes you are not minor matters. After taking into account the amount of time and energy a woman spends on her partner, it is only right that substantial attention be given back to her.

* * * * *

HANDLE WITH CARE

A cactus is a unique plant with conflicting characteristics. Protected by sharp thorns, the cactus also produces some of the most beautiful flowers of all. While a cactus will always have thorns for protection, flower production only occurs when the conditions are just right. Is your partner picking thorns from his hands or enjoying the flowers?

10. **Frequency and level of touch**

   a. Not touched at all or touched too much, ignored or groped
   b. Could use a lot more or a lot less touching
   c. Could use a little more or a little less touching
   d. Just right

11. **Does your partner flirt with you?**

   a. Yes
   b. No

12. **Personal hygiene of your partner and control of male habits (passing gas/burping/scratching)**

   a. He's a perfect gentleman
   b. There's room for improvement
   c. I have concerns
   d. I prefer the company of my cat

13. **Does your partner look at or comment about other women in your presence?**

   a. Not my man
   b. It happens but...
   c. Call a doctor I think his neck is broken

TANGO TIME

Ballroom dancing is a combination of leading and following. To be successful, a couple must master the art of communication and establish a form of trust. In order for the steps to become second nature, it requires a lot of time and practice. Is the tango an enjoyable activity with your partner, or are you attempting to dance with the man who has two left feet? Just in case he's not listening, let's spell it out in black and white.

14. Listening skills and comprehension

    a.   My partner listens and understands

    b.   My partner listens only

    c.   I talk to myself

15. **Is your partner a source of positive feedback and encouragement in your life?**

    a.   Yes

    b.   No

16. **Does your partner kiss and tell, or reveal aspects of your life to others you find hurtful?**

    a.   Yes, posing for Playboy would be less revealing

    b.   No, his lips are sealed

17. **Do you trust your partner?**

    a.   In all cases

    b.   Situational

    c.   No!!!!!!

....

"To be trusted is a greater
compliment than being loved."
~ George MacDonald

....

Make the Heart Race

It's a given your partner will make your heart race. Whether it's beating fast out of anger or happiness, will be influenced by your partner's actions. This segment explores some of the factors influencing your heart rate. Your partner's degree of thoughtfulness and expression of your importance to him are not minor matters. Does your partner have a heart of gold that moves you?

18. Do you receive gifts from your partner?

    a.   Yes, proceed to question 19

    b.   No, proceed to question 21 and enter (c.) for questions 19 and 20

19. Are gifts personal and a reflection of who you are as a person?

    a.   Yes, he knows me very well

    b.   No, not unless a thigh master counts

20. Are gifts given spontaneously and for no apparent reason?

    a.   Yes, he's very thoughtful

    b.   No, being struck by lightning is more probable

21. **Does your partner do little things for you? Gas up the car, take out the trash, pick up your dry cleaning, walk your dog, go grocery shopping, etc.**

    a.   Yes

    b.   What??? There are men who do these things?

22. **Does your partner say "Thank you" or show appreciation for the things you do for him?**

    a.   Yes

    b.   No

Bonus Question

23. **Do you like your partner's sense of humor?**

    a.   Yes

    b.   There are some moments I can't stand it

    c.   No, funerals get more laughs

* * * * *

Common Interest

This section examines factors either supporting or sabotaging your relationship. Some factors are unchangeable, while others can be improved upon if both partners are willing. Many of these factors can be used for relationship growth. It is essential that you and your partner are aware of these influences and how they impact your relationship.

* * * * *

FAMILY & YOU

This segment covers factors most likely to be intimately impacting your relationship. When in-laws, parents, and children are involved, a relationship can be tested. How well your relationship measures up will be influenced by factors not easily controlled. Do your family dynamics require a time out? Is family time one of your relationship's strengths? There are three different relationship scenarios, select the scenario that best matches your current relationship.

Dating, no children under the age of 18 involved

24. **What is your relationship with your potential future in-laws?**

   a.   Okay

   b.   Poor, like a comedy without the laughs

25. **Future family expectations?**

   a.   Same view on whether children are desired, if children are desired the number of children is compatible

   b.   Differing views on family plans

26. **Family?**

   a.   Both sets of parents are divorced

   b.   One set of parents is still married

   c.   Both sets of parents are married

Dating, children under the age of 18 involved

24. **What is your relationship with your potential future in-laws?**

    a.   Okay

    b.   Poor, time spent together is like time in prison

25. **Future family expectations?**

    a.   Same view on whether children are desired, if children are desired the number of children is compatible

    b.   Differing views on family plans

26. **Existing family dynamics**

    a.   Both partners have children, under the age of 18

    b.   One partner has children, under the age of 18

....

"Families are like fudge –
mostly sweet with a few nuts."
~ Author Unknown

....

Married

24. **What is your relationship with your in-laws?**

    a.   Okay

    b.   Poor, wolves and sheep can co-exist easier

25. **Future family expectations?**

    a.   Same view on whether children are desired, if children are desired the number of children is compatible

    b.   Differing views on family plans

26. **When was your last vacation together, three days or more *without* kids?**

    a.   Greater than two years ago

    b.   More than a year ago

    c.   Within the last twelve months

··

"When you look at your life, the greatest happinesses are family happinesses."
~ Joyce Brothers

··

RELIGION

Couples can struggle to find common ground when dealing with religion. What sounds like the harps of heaven to one partner may sound more like the slithering of snakes to the other. Some differences can be expected, but to what degree? Is your relationship seeing more "fire and brimstone" or "clouds and harps" when it comes to religion?

27. Is your partner tolerant of your religious beliefs?

    a.   Yes

    b.   No

28. Have you and your partner resolved in what faith any children, you have or may have, will be raised?

    a.   Yes

    b.   No

29. How do you feel about your partner's religious beliefs?

    a.   Okay

    b.   There are some issues

SHARED ACTIVITIES

This segment contains factors essential for a relationship's ongoing development. If something doesn't grow or change we call it a fossil – it's dead! Couples need to spend quality time together, sleeping and/or arguing don't count. Time is the greatest limiting factor. Are you taking the time to share things with your partner

30. Do you and your partner share a similar interest in one of the following; music, TV programs, or movies?

a.   Yes

b.   No

31. **Do you and your partner have a shared physical activity; such as bowling, golf, hiking, bird watching, etc?**

    a. Yes
    b. No

32. **Do you and your partner share similar political views?**

    a. Yes
    b. No

33. **Do you date, no kids or kid related activities?**

    a. Yes
    b. No, dating is something I hope to try again
        after the divorce

You've completed your portion of the evaluation; use the evaluation key on pages 104-105 to find the score. The second component of *Keeping Score*, "Knowledge is Power," starts on page 25 and provides a brief explanation of the factors and how they affect your relationship.

PART II

Knowledge is Power ~ Eve

Here's the best part of *Keeping Score* – it really is just common sense. We all possess common sense, but sometimes we just need a short refresher course. The following is a brief summary of the different factors and their relative importance. The biggest thing we can impact is knowledge, knowledge is power, and with knowledge you are empowered to improve your relationship.

* * * * *

BIG SWORD VS. BROKEN SWORD

The factors in this section are closely correlated as money is the common thread in all of them. Why does money matter so much? Because women say it does. Marilyn Monroe once said, "Money is to a man, what pretty is to a girl." Is it just coincidence online dating profiles for men tend to emphasize things like money and career? If you still think money doesn't matter, then perhaps you should respond to the profile of the guy still playing video games on his mother's couch.

Castle or Cave
Dollars or Pennies (Factor 1)

The reality is men with resources, or the ability to acquire resources, are more attractive to women. Money equals food, shelter, and security. While gold can't buy love, try to enjoy love without adequate financial means. Perhaps it is a biological influence, as pregnancy and child rearing can disrupt or limit the opportunities to advance financially. Unless a woman has abundant resources of her own, raising a family without the help of a partner can be an incredible challenge. Another influence might be cultural, as men for most of our world's history have held the vast majority of the assets. It would seem easier to marry your way to equality than to start from the bottom. With that said, remember the old saying, "Marry for money and you'll earn every penny!" The odds are both biological and cultural influences play a role. What's important is recognizing that money does matter and your relationship is affected by it.

Destructive Habitats (Factor 2)

People with destructive habits tend to have messy financial situations. While people can inherit large sums of money or benefit from a lucrative career, these same people are unlikely to retain their money for long. When it comes to destructive habits, the only real difference between those with money and those without money is the length of the party. If your partner has destructive habits, make sure his means are sufficient to provide for more than a weekend or two!

King or Squire

For some reason we almost want to give away money to well educated, highly motivated people with great personalities. We can also think of people we want to charge for simply consuming the air we might breathe. A low score in any one factor of this segment can be detrimental due to the highly correlated nature of these factors.

Education (Factor 3)

Education is the foundation from which opportunity springs. Job opportunities, promotions, and salaries often parallel the level of education your partner has acquired. Not only is his degree of education indicative of his future earning potential, but it serves to measure his level of competitiveness. In the cow herd today, a man without an education or any marketable skills is a steer. There is only one future in store for steers – shrink wrapped cuts of beef that must be sold before they start to stink.

Work Ethic (Factor 4)

We are all wired differently and over time some of these differences become more apparent than others. Individuals possessing a greater enthusiasm for work tend to advance faster and further than those who exhibit less excitement for the job at hand. In the long run this distinction can equate to a significant difference in job opportunities, promotions, and salaries. But it is not all about the money. Work can also give us a sense of purpose, a place in life, and allow us to socially interact with others. Individuals with a strong work ethic generally have better financial prospects, stronger social networks, and are thus more stable partners.

Behavior (Factor 5)

Polite behavior and consideration of others is the expected norm in our society (at least outside of politics). We can all remember the rude salesman, but do we remember the countless others who dutifully did their job? The difference in what we remember makes offensive behavior a big issue, even more important than the good behavior your partner may exhibit. Fortunately, this factor is correctable if your partner is willing to discuss it. Unfortunately, this factor is difficult to address, as most people are defensive about their behavior. They are either unaware of their quirks or they view them as indispensible aspects of their character. Your partner, in his portion of this evaluation, has been keyed to ask for your assistance in this area – "Dear, what is my fatal flaw?" Approach this factor with consideration and sensitivity.

Income Balance

Money matters are rarely just about money. Often issues surrounding money are the true source of tension. How well a couple can identify, address, and discuss these issues can influence the success of their relationship. If you and your partner have trouble talking about money, then you will most likely struggle talking about other important issues. Striking the right balance with these factors requires some very open discussions if a healthy relationship is desired.

Breadwinner (Factor 6)

This is not an easy factor to read about let alone talk over with a partner. So here goes, please hear me out before finding fault. Can you ever picture your father or a girlfriend saying, "Great, he's a wonderful man, he's lucky to have found you to provide for him." If that scenario makes you uncomfortable, it also makes men squirm. This factor can be split into two separate issues. One, how women who earn more than their partner view the relationship, and, secondly, how their partner views the relationship.

Women are competitive, especially when it comes to partners with the ability to deliver financially. A portion of your own sense of value is likely linked to the financial capacity of the partner you have chosen. Our society places a premium on financial matters. If your partner doesn't measure up financially, there will be some wondering, "What's wrong with her?" Society and others outside of the relationship may imply you have "settled." After all, if you've made it to the top so handily, then why hasn't your partner done so as well? Does it really matter who makes more money? From a strictly financial point of view, no. Money can be saved or spent the same, regardless of who earns it. Society and traditional values, however, make this factor a real source of relationship pain and frustration. This factor is basically a no-win situation, as women who earn less than their partner may still feel less valued if their partner is not a high income earner.

For your partner, things are a bit more straightforward, the bias is unlikely to be disguised. Historically in our society the man has been the breadwinner, at least that is how it has been portrayed. The idea of the woman "bringing home the bacon," let alone more bacon than the man, is a fairly new one. Men who earn less than their partners tend to be viewed in a negative light by society. These men are often considered lazy, leeches, or dependents. If one of society's traditional roles has been for the man to be the breadwinner and you can do it better, what do you think his view of the relationship is likely to be?

Just to make sure you understand me without the possibility of misunderstanding – women should feel comfortable earning as much or more than their partners. As men will never apologize for earning more than women, neither should you, if that is the case. We are moving from a physical labor set of job skills to an information based set of job skills. Given the higher percentages of women earning college degrees than men, it is obvious the financial balance (in relationships) is going to be reset.

What really matters is that you are fully aware of the significance of the "breadwinner" issue. Recognize that this factor does play a role in your relationship and that it does have impacts. The effects of societal and cultural pressures can subtly undermine a relationship and should not be underestimated. The goal is to have couples comfortable discussing money issues and for both partners to feel secure about their financial role in the relationship.

Balance (Factor 7)

A healthy relationship requires a good balance with work. As every relationship will have different financial goals, so every relationship will have a different balance. Be sure to think longer term with this factor. Just because your partner has been working seventy hours a week for the last two months or is currently unemployed doesn't mean things are necessarily out of balance. The real question may be how chronic is this situation? It may also be time to review how well your financial needs and goals align with reality. A proper balance may require walks in the park once a week instead of Paris in the spring. Time at work means less time for other things.

Equality (Factor 8)

Equality is very important, as we all desire a sense of justice and fairness. This is not necessarily a factor that will have a hard and fast answer, as this is something we feel. It may be possible one of you works full time, while the other cares for the children. Both sides may feel they have the harder job and, as it's a personal viewpoint, both sides can be right. The solution here is to acknowledge one another's views regarding this factor. In cases where one party feels abused, work to find a more equitable solution.

Financial Planning (Factor 9)

Fights over financial matters are a leading cause of relationship failure, which is unfortunate, as solutions to financial problems are readily available. If the relationship really matters to you, then the next book you read should be about financial planning. Many couples struggle with financial matters due to a lack of experience and education with financial issues. The goal is to avoid fighting over finances. This is accomplished through communication and trust. Both of which are the end products of jointly developing financial goals and a plan relating to money management. There are numerous ways for couples to successfully structure their finances, but you've got to start by having the conversation. If you and your partner are effectively communicating about financial matters there will be far fewer unpleasant revelations and less conflict.

A quick note for our single readers. Not only is the development of a joint financial plan a good idea prior to marriage, but it also makes the transition to married life easier. A few things you should be willing to share with your partner and insist upon having shared with you in return, would include credit scores and a total disclosure of debt. The seventy-five thousand dollars worth of student loans acquired while obtaining a masters degree in Middle Age Saxon adverbs may have a chilling effect on your passion. Keep your finances separate until you have reached a level of commitment requiring you to mingle money. Go in with the full knowledge of what you are taking on, eyes wide open. This is not an area that comes with many pleasant surprises!

TRIED & TRUE

Interestingly enough in the trials that helped shape *Keeping Score*, the results were quite consistent in this section. Women in troubled relationships would either have nearly perfect scores or exceptionally low scores in this section. A perfect score in this section was often undermined by very low scores in Big Sword vs Broken Sword; women choosing partners who met their emotional needs, but struggled financially. Low scores in this section were usually consistent with high scores in Big Sword vs Broken Sword; women selecting partners who focused on career and financial success, but neglected the nurturing aspects of a relationship.

Handle with Care

A great deal of the physical intimacy expressed in a relationship can be traced to the factors making up this segment. It's been said, "Men just need a place, women need a reason." If these factors are reasonably answered it may be time to consider a place!

Touch (Factor 10)

There is no right or wrong way to touch, there's just your way or the highway! Touch is about personal preference and unless you are making your views known, don't expect much improvement. Even if it's just right, let him know so he has some idea that he is pleasing you. This is not an area you want to leave to your partner's friends or his late night television programs.

Flirting (Factor 11)

Flirting is defined as making playfully romantic or sexual overtures to someone you find attractive. I imagine when you first met your partner, flirting came quite easily to the both of you. Often, over time, we forget to flirt with our partners. No matter how long a relationship has been going on, a woman still desires the approval of her partner; she needs to feel attractive. Simply put, flirting makes everyone feel good. If you're not being flirted with, perhaps you need to initiate the exchange and revive your relationship. Or consider the possibility that you might be sending signals discouraging your partner from flirting with you. A remark attributed to Mae West sums things up nicely, "It is better to be looked over than overlooked."

Hygiene (Factor 12)

Most women are raised from birth to take personal hygiene matters very seriously. Men, well, there's a reason the question was asked. One of the most common complaints of women in relationship counseling is they don't like the smell of their partner. Just as a skunk may not find its odor offensive, men can be equally oblivious. Basic hygiene becomes even more important as a man ages. Want to know how old a man is? Unless he's well groomed, you simply just need to look for ear and nose hair! In most cases, men are unaware of the need for improved grooming practices and are willing to change their daily routine if it helps them to be more attractive. Just remember to tactfully approach the subject.

Control of male habits is a serious topic. Most of these actions are standard operating procedure in the company of male friends, and that is where they belong. If you have not expressed your distaste for this behavior, then it is time you two had a talk. Excuses may include, "It's a sign I'm comfortable with you" or "I forgot," but make sure your partner understands the importance of controlling these actions in your presence. Surely your partner doesn't indulge in these bodily actions in the presence of his grandmother or during a job interview? A "yes" answer probably explains why he is unemployed living in a van <u>outside</u> his mother's house! Respect is what you are after.

Other Women (Factor 13)

Let's start by clearing the air – all men look at or talk about other women, yes, even yours. It's how he first noticed you, so be thankful.

Men are like dogs. All dogs have the genetics to hunt. The question is whether you have a yellow lab wagging its tail at the mail woman or a hound dog baying all night at the cats in the alley. In both cases, the problem is that you have to see it or hear it. So what are the options? Shock collar treatment, let him run wild, neuter him, or should you just put this mongrel down? Though some of these options may sound appealing, what you need to determine is whether or not your dog is trainable. Your partner needs to know how much his behavior hurts you and, if he values you, he will learn to better control these impulses.

Tango Time

Certain dances require specific musical counts. You are not going to be able to Salsa to the beat of most classical music. Getting the steps right can be frustrating. Every relationship will have its own moves and rhythm. It's going to take time, practice, and persistence if your relationship is going to flow with the factors in this segment.

Communication (Factor 14)

Women and men communicate very differently. When men talk they tend to be bragging about something or trying to find an answer to a problem, in both cases a boost to their ego. Women are more likely to talk as a means of sharing. They want someone to listen, empathize, and relate. Sure, there are men who nail this factor; the problem is they have a life span of about two hours. Outside of the movies, these men are about as common as women who enjoy childbirth! In order to communicate more effectively with your partner, you must understand the differences in the way men and women speak to one another. Communication is a learned skill that takes time and patience, but even more so when it comes to the opposite sex.

Encouragement (Factor 15)

A partner should be someone who provides you with positive feedback and encouragement. It is important that your partner is able to help identify your strengths and weaknesses without diminishing your self-confidence. Whether it's dealing with a two year old refusing to be potty trained or applying for your dream job that has just opened up, encouragement from you partner can make all the difference. We all have self-doubt, but a supportive partner can help push you forward.

Kiss and Tell (Factor 16)

There are some things that are not to be shared outside of your relationship. For most people this is understood, but there are those who need the boundaries to be clarified. Neither partner should indulge others with sensitive information that would either embarrass or hurt the other. Shared moments between you and your partner are what make your relationship special. The betrayal of this trust can cause irreparable damage. There can be considerable confusion as to what specific aspects of your life are not subject to public disclosure. It is best to draw the lines clearly.

Trust (Factor 17)

Trust can take forever to earn and can be broken quickly. Broken trust is a subject *Keeping Score* is incapable of exploring in any great depth for it is a heavy subject that falls outside of quick and easy solutions. If your answer implies that you do not fully trust your partner, then the lack of trust is likely founded in either a past relationship or a more recent event. If broken trust from a past relationship is causing doubt in your current relationship, then it would benefit you to share this information with your partner. Discuss ways in which your partner can alleviate your anxiety and give you reassurance. If a recent event has raised your suspicions, then you should discuss your concerns with your partner. Some environments encourage risky behavior and a practical compromise may involve avoiding challenging atmospheres – less time at Bikini Beach and more time in a soup kitchen for the homeless.

Make the Heart Race

Relationships without heart pounding moments and pleasant memories to fall back on tend to have bleak futures. When a couple shares a positive experience with each another, the effect can last for years, even decades. Often these powerful memories are what carry a couple through the ups and downs of a relationship. While these moments may be brief in nature, their power can be everlasting. Whether your relationship has a healthy pulse or is on life support can be partially explained here.

Gifts (Factor 18)

Gifts are a measure of affection and appreciation, not a payment for services (that's what Visa is for). Men have several approaches to gift giving and are often hurtfully wrong. Here are a few helpful hints for your partner: no gifts suggesting you are less than perfect (ex. exercise equipment or self-help books – *Keeping Score*), no gifts he will enjoy more than you, no appliances or other household items (unless you specifically asked for it), and when it comes to clothing, unless your partner knows your exact size, just don't buy it! His focus should be on creating a positive memory, not just giving a gift.

Some men are reluctant to give gifts due to the pressure created by mass industries to "prove" their love and a genuine fear of giving a gift below their partner's expectations. Therefore, it is important that when your partner does get it wrong, you don't make a big issue of it. Perhaps in time, you both may be able to look back on the moment with fondness and laughter, creating a positive memory. Remember that gift giving is a choice and criticizing your partner's choice of gifts may lead to no gifts at all.

True Gifts (Factor 19)

A gift that is personal and a reflection of who you are is called a "true gift." These are the gifts that deeply move you and touch your heart. True gifts are powerful because they show that the giver has taken the time to get to know you and what holds meaning for you. In order to pick a true gift, it requires an intimate knowledge that is only gained through time, experience, and keen observation. There are few shortcuts to hasten your partner's ability to identify what is special or has significant meaning to you. Your partner may require some direction to accomplish this; dropping subtle hints (or not so subtle) might improve the odds!

Surprise Gifts (Factor 20)

If you already know you'll be receiving a gift or know what the gift is, then there is no real surprise. What's the fun in that? Gifts given on Valentine's Day or your birthday are examples of obligatory gifts, gifts that are expected. Your partner understands the penalties involved with failing to comply with these expected tokens of appreciation. That's what makes unexpected gifts such a treat – someone was thinking about you when they didn't have to.

Little Things (Factor 21)

Often it is the "little things" that we do or don't do in a relationship that make or break it. Over a period of time, the little things add up and can make you happier than any material gift your partner may buy you. Think of the feeling you would have leaving for work in the morning in a warmed up car with a full tank of gas or coming home after a long day to a cooked meal and a clean kitchen. Can you really put a price on such things? If your partner is already doing these things than consider yourself lucky and be thankful. Little things are done out of love and consideration and it is important to appreciate them, not expect them. Be careful not to turn these little tasks into chores for him or let him know the kitchen wasn't cleaned to your standards. If it turns into a job neither of you will get the same satisfaction from seeing these things done. This is a chance for him to demonstrate he cares about you and provide you with unlimited pleasant surprises in the future.

Appreciation (Factor 22)

Your partner's failure to show appreciation for the things you do for him is the quickest way for these actions to disappear. If we were properly raised the words "please" and "thank you" should be standard parts of our vocabulary. Some men are in need of basic manners. Some men simply need a refresher course. If you aren't receiving appreciation for the things you do because your partner has come to expect them as standard, then he may have to do them on his own for awhile. Men often forget the time and effort it takes to complete the many little things women do for them. Remind him how a simple "please" and "thank you" are much appreciated.

Bonus Question
(Factor 23)

Humor can make a man more attractive. Women attribute numerous qualities to men viewed as having a good sense of humor; such as greater sensitivity, intelligence, confidence, and masculinity. Humor even seems to make men appear taller. Aside from the obvious qualities just mentioned, there are a few other overlooked aspects regarding your man's sense of humor. If you are laughing or at least amused by him, you are going to find it harder to hold the numerous things he has done wrong against him for very long. Your partner's humor can often diffuse difficult situations and lighten the mood during sensitive moments. These kinds of men are entertaining and fun to be around. With that said, not all humor is appreciated or appropriate. If there are some instances where you find his humor out of line, he needs to know.

COMMON INTEREST

Think of your relationship like a garden. First you must choose the proper plot of land, then you carefully plan your garden, and finally you sow the seeds with realistic expectations of the site's potential. As the garden grows you must maintain it. If a garden isn't periodically weeded, weeds can take over and consume the nutrients your crop needs. Failure to fertilize and provide adequate water for your garden may not kill it, but the harvest is likely to be disappointing. Not only will you reap what you sow in the end, but there are numerous factors that either increase the yield or contribute to crop failure.

Family & You

The garden-relationship example fits this segment very well. You are not likely to be starting out with a bare plot of earth. There are apt to be trees and flower beds already well established in the garden. While you will have your own plans and varieties you want to plant, the space allotted to you may come with pre-existing conditions. In addition, there may be some species in need of a pruning or requiring the construction of a barrier to keep them out of your space. A firm grasp of the lay of the land will make your efforts much more likely to bear fruit.

In-laws (Factor 24)

There are countless movies where interactions with the in-laws are portrayed as humorous. Unfortunately, real life just isn't that funny and some of you are probably still waiting for a happy ending. If you answered your relationship was "okay" then your in-laws are likely impacting your relationship in a positive way by either supporting the relationship or by not detracting from it. Consider yourself fortunate and be mindful of ways to maintain this relationship. If you answered "poor" then the subject of in-laws can get complicated. A poor relationship with your in-laws not only affects you, but your partner as well. If you think your relationship with your in-laws is difficult, then imagine the position your partner is in. It isn't easy keeping both sides happy.

There may be numerous reasons why your relationship with your in-laws may be less than perfect. These reasons can include personal history, race, religion, education, culture, or simply a clash of personalities. Sometimes these differences can be extremely difficult to resolve. It is important to remember you cannot change your in-laws or how they think; you can only control your own behavior and your reaction to them.

So how do you deal with a poor relationship with your in-laws? There are no easy answers here, as each relationship is unique. Complete avoidance of your in-laws may sound appealing, but is probably unrealistic. Keeping the peace may not always be possible, but you will have better control of the outcome if you and your partner discuss how to handle the conflict beforehand. This at least keeps peace in your relationship and gives you and your partner a united front. Sometimes, a quick "Mom and Dad, your actions are hurting my relationship. If you care about me you will stop doing this," may suffice. Generally, it's not your role to take on your in-laws; it's your partner's job. You can only control your own actions and often the best course of action is simply tolerance.

Future Family Expectations (Factor 25)

Whether you are thinking minivan or a couples Harley, hopefully you and your partner share a similar vision on family planning. Children are one of life's greatest gifts and are often a fundamental part of relationships. That said, children can also be one of life's greatest sources of stress and financial worry. Family planning should not be avoided or ignored. If differences exist, there needs to be a discussion which is open and honest.

We all have personal preferences that should be respected. The emotional, physical, and financial commitments involved with children make this a factor where compromise may not always be possible. If the differences are substantial, your time will be better spent finding a partner with views that parallel your own.

Family – dating with no children under 18 (Factor 26)

Considering the high divorce rate in our society, the odds are (between you and your partner) at least one set of parents will be divorced. Why does this factor matter? Just as communication between two people can be problematic, increasing the number of people involved only further complicates matters. If both sets of parents are still married, you and your partner only have four other people to try to please. If both sets of parents are divorced and have remarried, you and your partner have a potential of eight people to please. Is it really enjoyable trying to split Christmas among four different homes? These outside pressures tend to spill over into your relationship as well. In this case, fewer people equals fewer conflicts, which is never a bad thing for a relationship.

Another underappreciated benefit from having parents that are still married comes in the form of positive role models. Not only can parents provide proof it is possible to stay married, they may even have some insights that can be helpful to your own relationship. While your parents may have separated or failed to provide what could be considered an example of a healthy relationship, that doesn't absolve you from trying. This evaluation should have brought up some ideas as to how your relationship could function more effectively. It's up to you and your partner if someday *your* kids and grandkids will be trying to emulate *your* relationship.

Whether your parents are divorced or married, the reality is parents can cause problems for relationships. You and your partner need to develop a parent plan, ensuring your relationship comes first. Pleasing your parents is somewhere after that.

Family – dating with children under 18 involved (Factor 26)

There is no doubt children are an incredible source of joy in a relationship. However, the problems associated with combining children from past relationships into a new family structure can turn that joy into heartache. Combining families is not to be taken lightly. As the old saying goes, "Blood is thicker than water." As conflicts arise, finding solutions all parties will find satisfactory and equitable can be challenging. The odds are better if only one partner has children under eighteen, but it's still not an easy path. Mixed families can be successful, though they require a lot of hard work, good communication, and additional education. If your relationship fits in this category it would be beneficial to educate yourself. There are well written books and sources on the internet that offer sound advice; you are not the first person with this situation. Be sure to approach this factor with a lot of thought and consideration.

Vacations (*Married*, Factor 26)

A friend of mine once commented, "What is it about kids that suck all the joy out of a woman?" While this is a harsh statement, it does emphasize the importance for couples to spend time alone together without the interruptions of children or other demands. "Couples only" vacations are essential for relationship growth and healing. It is a time to revert to your former self and see your partner as the person you fell in love with. A time absent of emails, business calls, conferences, and other distractions of daily life. The family trip to Grandma's house or the company summer retreat just doesn't count!

Religion
(Factors 27-29)

Religion is a deeply personal factor that everyone experiences in a different way. Wherever strong emotions are mixed with personal preferences, the potential for extreme conflict exists. There are cases where both couples share the same religious beliefs, but have differing levels of spiritual intensity and still find this issue explosive.

Religious conflict can be fatal to a relationship due to its sensitive nature. The best option is to avoid a relationship where extreme differences in religious beliefs are involved. The only other option is to develop tolerance and make a point of keeping religion at a distance when it comes to your relationship. The damage that occurs to a relationship trying to settle a religious dispute may be too destructive for the relationship to survive the process or aftermath. Even if your relationship is currently experiencing religious harmony, watch this factor closely. People change as they mature and significant events in life (birth of a child, death of a parent) can bring about sudden shifts in beliefs.

Shared Activities

This is the segment where you learn to fertilize and water your garden. It's not just enough to plant and weed. You have to encourage growth every chance you can. As relationships are a living entity, they are capable of growth and healing when the conditions are right. Optimal growing conditions do not happen by chance, they require the knowledge and skills of a good gardener.

Interests & Activities (Factors 30, 31)

Finding things both you and your partner can enjoy together is important. Part of the fun can be doing new things together as you search for something to share. If you both enjoy something you are more likely to spend time together. The activity or interest isn't nearly as important as the time shared. Just the act of being together allows for other positive experiences to occur. Whether it's small talk, holding hands, or a kiss that leads somewhere – none of these things are a possibility when you are pursuing separate interests.

Beliefs & Values (Factor 32)

When someone reaffirms a belief or view you hold, it generates a positive feeling towards that person. Positive feelings create a connection between you and your partner, further strengthening your bond. Even in cases where you may enjoy a spirited discussion of an issue, it still pays to find areas where you can agree with one another. If agreement is impossible, then you need to develop tolerance which is a process by itself.

Dating (Factor 33)

We usually think of dating as something we do at the start of a relationship. What is the purpose of a date? A date is an opportunity to showcase your best attributes and see what your companion has to offer. Dating can be viewed as a sales job. In the context of a relationship the sales pitch should never end as the product is returnable! Dating provides an opportunity outside of everyday life for couples to remember why they are together and form new memories. It chops, dices, slices, and now it also spices!!! Think sales, do you remember why you brought this product home?

You have now completed the second component of *"Keeping Score"* and are ready for the third component "A Score to Win" starting on page 97.

PART I

Adam

Let me start with an apology, as this evaluation is likely preventing you from doing something else you really want to do. It is quite probable your partner purchased this book and you are now expected to read *Keeping Score* as part of seeing how the relationship is functioning. Look at the bright side of things. First, the fact your partner has you doing this evaluation indicates she places some value on you, how much value we have yet to see. Second, the time spent with this book will be far more enjoyable than similar time spent in counseling or with a divorce attorney. Third, consider what this book costs in comparison to the services mentioned above – that alone should make you smile. With these thoughts in your mind let's get started. Who knows, it might even be fun!

> ➤ Use the relationship evaluation forms on pages 113-116 to record your answers. Refer to page 108 for an example of how to use the evaluation forms.

Wonder Woman

Men are physical. To like a woman we need to like what we see. What do the words, "She has a great personality," tell you? Not that it's likely you are in a relationship with a woman who has to wear a paper bag over her head, but the happier you are with her physique the better the relationship will be. How a woman looks is by no means written in stone. While some aspects of a woman's appearance are unchangeable, much of it can be modified. The female gender has perfected the art of the makeover. Has your partner mastered this game or is there some room for improvement?

* * * * *

THE GOODS

Her physical features caught your attention in the beginning, before you gave much thought to her other qualities. While her physical appearance is still important to you, it's probably even more important to her. We are all judged on our physical appearance. Women, however, are held to a higher standard than men. These attributes of your partner are not easy to alter. Be sure to really think through your answers.

1. **Do you like your partner's facial features and use of accessories? Take into account makeup, glasses, earrings, beauty marks, piercings, etc. Do you like what you see or would you like to see some changes?**
   a. Perfect
   b. Minor changes desired
   c. Some changes desired
   d. Big changes desired

2. **With a range from 32AA to 46EE and beyond, what's your perfect fit? Use a bit of reality and sensitivity here, as nothing escapes the forces of gravity. The real question is, are you happy with what she has to offer?**

   a. Perfect
   b. Minor changes desired
   c. Some changes desired
   d. Big changes desired

3. **What is the condition of your partner's tail end? How do your partner's "assets" compare with your preference in this area? Some men like a tight end, others like some junk in the trunk. To each his own. How's the scenery from your viewpoint?**

   a. Perfect
   b. Minor changes desired
   c. Some changes desired
   d. Big changes desired

....

"Beauty comes in all sizes, not just size 5."
~ Roseanne

....

Hair

Around the world and across cultures a woman's hair is considered a prized possession. The extreme attention women's hair receives is evident in the amount of shelf space grocery stores dedicate to hair products, the number of weeks in advance women have to book hair appointments, and the fact women have bad hair days. You are likely to have some preferences in regard to how your partner's hair looks. Do you like blondes, brunettes, short hair, curly hair, etc? Keep in mind you can't have one of each!

4.   <u>Length</u> – **Do you like the length of your partner's hair? Would you like it longer or shorter? Rate it.**

   a.   Perfect
   b.   Minor changes desired
   c.   Some changes desired
   d.   Big changes desired

5. **Color – Do you like your partner's hair color? There are so many different colors available, selecting just one may be a problem. Is there any particular color you really find attractive?**

   a. Perfect
   b. Minor changes desired
   c. Some changes desired
   d. Big changes desired

6. **Style – How much do you like your partner's current hair style? Does it fit her personality well, is it age appropriate, profession appropriate, or can it be improved upon?**

   a. Perfect
   b. Minor changes desired
   c. Some changes desired
   d. Big changes desired

....

"I'm not offended by all the dumb-blonde jokes because I know that I'm not dumb.
I also know I'm not blonde."

~ Dolly Parton

....

Armor

Clothing is the armor women wear in the world. Armor is designed to protect the person wearing it and should fit the person well if it's to be effective. Good clothing can make a woman feel more confident by accentuating her positive attributes while concealing her weaknesses. There are good reasons why women spend so much time shopping and why a perfect outfit is to die for. Some women can pull together a strong suit of armor; others may need a little help. View this as a chance to help your partner, but be realistic. Wearing high heels and fishnet stockings seven days a week is not practical, no matter how much you may desire it.

7. <u>**Everyday wear**</u> **– Your partner's selection and use of everyday clothing is?**
    a. Perfect
    b. Minor changes desired
    c. Some changes desired
    d. Big changes desired

8. **Special occasion – Your partner's selection and use of special occasion clothing is?**

    a. Perfect
    b. Minor changes desired
    c. Some changes desired
    d. Big changes desired

9. **Intimate wear – Your partner's selection and use of intimate wear is?**

    a. Perfect
    b. Minor changes desired
    c. Some changes desired
    d. Big changes desired

··

"A dress that zips up the back
will bring a husband and wife together."
~ James H. Boren

··

Soul

This section is about the essence of a woman. If it is a good match with a man, the relationship is less likely to cause problems in his life. There are three segments in this section designed to identify areas of potential conflict and levels of comfort. A woman can have all the goods you like, but if the soul is a poor match you'll find the goods a whole lot less enjoyable. Think of it like a car. You can admire a Lamborghini, but would you like paying the insurance, worrying about scratching it, and is it really something you'd want to take grocery shopping? This section gets into how good a fit this relationship is with your life.

* * * * *

FINANCIAL

Financial issues are a leading cause of relationship conflict. The choices you and your partner make relating to money matters will play a large role in your relationship. This segment impacts today and far into the future. It's worth taking the time to get it right.

10. **What is your partner's attitude towards debt, savings, and investments in comparison to your own beliefs?**

    a. Don't know
    b. Similar views
    c. Opposing views

11. **Are you financially capable of providing the lifestyle your partner desires?**

    a. Yes
    b. Don't know
    c. No

12. **Do you trust your partner with financial matters?**

    a. Yes, one street wise woman
    b. It depends
    c. No, it's either a bubble about to pop or a crash in progress

NURTURE

This segment is a hard one to express. The best description I've developed so far is how would the <u>perfect</u> mother treat you? The perfect mother in the movies always has Junior's favorite meal on the table, there's no problem too big to share with mother, never a worry about your socks matching, and if you are sick it's a sad moment when you recover. By now we all should have been weaned, but after a day playing with the big boys there is still something about being pampered we can't resist.

13. <u>**Cooking**</u> **– Do you get special meals? How happy are you with what's on the menu?**

    a.   She can cook?

    b.   It's good

    c.   I clean the plate and ask for seconds

14. <u>**Household**</u> **– Do you like her style of decorating? Cleanliness? Is this a place you feel comfortable in?**

    a.   Like her approach

    b.   I'm okay with it

    c.   There are some issues

Factors relating to Nurture
for <u>single</u> men only

15. <u>**Confidence**</u> **– How comfortable are you sharing personal details with your partner? This includes health issues, problems at work, issues involving your family or friends.**

   a. Very open
   b. Hesitant
   c. We don't go there

16. <u>**Dependence**</u> **– Does your partner interact with you at a comfortable level? If not, is your partner too clingy or does your partner give you more space than you want?**

   a. Just right
   b. Won't complain
   c. There are some problems
   d. This is not healthy

Factors relating to Nurture
for __married__ men only

15. __Harmony__ – How well does your partner complement your life? Does your partner do the little things that make your day run smoothly? Things that you are apt not to notice until they are not done (ex. buying your socks, paying the bills, etc...).

    a. Highly complementary
    b. Some improvement possible
    c. Frustrated

16. __Royalty factor__ – Do you get any special treatment when you're sick? Does your partner show appreciation for what you do or recognize your efforts? Is your partner someone who sympathizes or relates to the stresses in your life? Does she listen to you?

    a. I'm the King
    b. I'm the Prince
    c. I'm the Butler
    d. I'm the dirt beneath her feet

LOYALTY

This segment is about a man having peace of mind and how secure he is in the relationship. A relationship needs a foundation that includes a healthy level of trust. Without the sense of security that comes from trust, a relationship is not going to give you peace of mind.

17. **"Stand by your man" factor.**

    a. Stands by you in public and makes sure your faults are constructively discussed in private

    b. Stands by you in public but either ignores your shortcomings or fails to address your faults in a constructive manner in private

    c. Will expose your shortcomings in public

18. **Given the perfect opportunity do you think your partner is likely to cheat on you?**

    a. Yes

    b. Unsure

    c. No

19. Do your friends like your partner?

    a.   Yes

    b.   No

20. Does your partner have girlfriends with good character?

    a.   Yes

    b.   So/So

    c.   No

Bonus Question

21. Will your partner let your past shortcomings go or are you reminded of these moments regularly?

    a.   Partner has an excellent memory, my mistakes are a regular topic in our conversations

    b.   Most of the time mistakes I've made are forgotten, every so often I get to hear about them all over again

    c.   So long as I'm not repeating the same mistake it remains forgotten

* * * * *

Common Interest

This section examines factors either supporting or sabotaging your relationship. Some factors are unchangeable, while others can be improved upon if both partners are willing. Many of these factors can be used for relationship growth. It is essential that you and your partner are aware of these influences and how they impact your relationship.

* * * * *

FAMILY & YOU

This segment covers factors most likely to be intimately impacting your relationship. When in-laws, parents, and children are involved, a relationship can be tested. How well your relationship measures up will be influenced by factors not easily controlled. Do your family dynamics require a time out? Is family time one of your relationship's strengths? There are three different relationship scenarios below, select the scenario that best matches your current relationship.

- Dating, no children under the age of 18 involved, page – 69
- Dating, children under the age of 18 involved, page – 70
- Married, page – 71

Dating, no children under the age of 18 involved

22. What is your relationship with your potential future in-laws?

a. Okay

b. Poor, like a comedy without the laughs

23. Future family expectations?

a. Same view on whether children are desired, if children are desired the number of children is compatible

b. Differing views on family plans

24. Family?

a. Both sets of parents are divorced

b. One set of parents is still married

c. Both sets of parents are married

Dating, children under the age of 18 involved

22. **What is your relationship with your potential future in-laws?**
    a. Okay
    b. Poor, time spent together is like time in prison

23. **Future family expectations?**
    a. Same view on whether children are desired, if children are desired the number of children is compatible
    b. Differing views on family plans

24. **Existing family dynamics**
    a. Both partners have children, under the age of 18
    b. One partner has children, under the age of 18

....

"The great gift of family life is to be intimately acquainted with people you might never even introduce yourself to, had life not done it for you."
~ Kendall Hailey

....

Married

22. What is your relationship with your in-laws?

    a.   Okay

    b.   Poor, wolves and sheep can co-exist easier

23. Future family expectations?

    a.   Same view on whether children are desired, if children are desired the number of children is compatible

    b.   Differing views on family plans

24. When was your last vacation together, three days or more *without* kids?

    a.   Greater than two years ago

    b.   More than a year ago

    c.   Within the last twelve months

....

"The most important thing a father can do
for his children is to love their mother."
~ Theodore Hesburgh

....

RELIGION

Couples can struggle to find common ground when dealing with religion. What sounds like the harps of heaven to one partner may sound more like the slithering of snakes to the other. Some differences can be expected, but to what degree? Is your relationship seeing more "fire and brimstone" or "clouds and harps" when it comes to religion?

25. Is your partner tolerant of your religious beliefs?

    a.   Yes

    b.   No

26. Have you and your partner resolved in what faith any children, you have or may have, will be raised?

    a.   Yes

    b.   No

27. How do you feel about your partner's religious beliefs?

    a.   Okay

    b.   There are some issues

SHARED ACTIVITIES

This segment contains factors essential for a relationship's ongoing development. If something doesn't grow or change we call it a fossil – it's dead! Couples need to spend quality time together, sleeping and/ or arguing don't count. Time is the greatest limiting factor. Are you taking the time to share things with your partner?

28. **Do you and your partner share a similar interest in one of the following; music, TV programs, or movies?**

   a.   Yes

   b.   No

29. **Do you and your partner have a shared physical activity; such as bowling, golf, hiking, bird watching, etc?**

    a.   Yes

    b.   No

30. **Do you and your partner share similar political views?**

    a.   Yes

    b.   No

31. **Do you date, no kids or kid related activities?**

    a.   Yes

    b.   No, dating is something I hope to try again after the divorce

You've completed your portion of the evaluation; use the evaluation key on pages 106-107 to find the score. The second component of *Keeping Score*, "Knowledge is Power," starts on page 75 and provides a brief explanation of the factors and how they affect your relationship.

PART II

Knowledge is Power – Adam

Here's the best part of *Keeping Score* – it really is just common sense. We all possess common sense, but sometimes we just need a short refresher course. The following is a brief summary of the different factors and their relative importance. The biggest thing we can impact is knowledge, knowledge is power, and with knowledge you are empowered to improve your relationship.

* * * * *

WONDER WOMAN

Why is it so important men like what they see? There are some strong biological considerations at work here. A woman's physical features are indicators of her fertility. There are subconscious forces working to shape what you consider your personal preferences. Even if you have no intention of fathering children with a woman, there are biological aspects of your nature hoping otherwise! The behavior of women makes this case even stronger. Most women spend a significant amount of time trying to maintain a youthful appearance, which is also related to fertility. The majority of women seem to dedicate their efforts to looking somewhere between 20-45 years of age, with an emphasis on younger being better.

The Goods
(Factors 1-3)

The physical attributes of a woman are largely off limits, they are what they are. Things like glasses, the spring break 2004 tattoo, or use of makeup can be discussed in a delicate manner. Given the amount of attention a woman gives to her looks, be careful not to harshly criticize your partner on her choices. The demands modern society places on women (childcare, work, household chores) often leave little time for self improvement. Are you willing to take on some of the workload so that your partner has time for a facial or workout session? Even better yet, if time allows, why not join your partner for some self-improvement measures? Our society has some unrealistic expectations about what a woman should look like; it has not been healthy for either gender. In the end if she's smiling and is happy to be with you, then what's your problem?

Hair
(Factors 4-6)

Hair can be changed if your partner knows what you like. While you have been free here to analyze her hair choice and make suggestions, don't make a habit of it. Remember, how a woman feels about herself can often be related to the condition of her hair. Above all, notice when she gets her hair done and find something nice to say about it. It really is an effort to make herself more attractive to you.

Armor
(Factors 7-9)

There's no easy way to influence how a woman dresses, or more honestly, no cheap way. If you want to see some changes in her closet, be prepared to spend some money. Go shopping with her. This way you'll be sure to get her sizes correct (write them down for future use) and you'll learn something about putting outfits together. Once you have her sizes and a sense of her style, you are ready to go alone. Trust me when I say there are plenty of saleswomen willing to assist you; they are very good at helping you spend your money! For those of you who are content with your partner's armor, this is still a good exercise. Depending on how your partner scores you, it may very well become your next new hobby.

Soul

In the field exercises that helped shape *Keeping Score*, this is where things started to fall apart for men. In numerous cases, the woman would have a perfect score in the Wonder Woman section, but the relationship would crash here. In short, the man was fixated on the physical, with nothing to sustain the relationship beyond that. We see this kind of activity on the Nature Channel or the Call of the Wild. Real relationships with real women require more than just a physical attraction. What works for squirrels is not applicable for humans. So unless you have doubts about your chromosome count, continue reading.

Financial

Some people will ignore the strange noise a car is making, so long as it keeps moving. Many relationships disregard financial matters until the problem becomes impossible to ignore. This approach ensures that when the bank accounts are empty, the patience and understanding needed to fix the situation will also be overdrawn. Ignoring the strange sound a car is making only increases the repair bill or may even damage the car beyond repair. Whether your relationship is headed for the junk yard or the Indy 500 depends on you and your partner's financial attitude and planning.

Financial (Factor 10)

Financial matters need to be grounded in a cold hard reality; there is no room for soft fuzzy feelings here. A good place to start is to know what you and your partner's beliefs are towards money matters. When financial problems arise in a relationship, it is largely due to incompatible financial practices. There are couples happily living paycheck to paycheck in addition to being on a first name basis with the pawnshop. The key factor seems to be that neither partner minds living this way. Ideally it's best if you and your partner have similar financial attitudes. Most relationships have some differences, but these differences don't have to be sources of conflict. If you place any value on your relationship, the next book you read after this one should be about financial planning. A financial plan developed together will recognize your differences and incorporate strategies designed to prevent these differences from becoming areas of conflict.

A quick note for our single readers. Not only is the development of a joint financial plan a good idea prior to marriage, it also makes the transition to married life easier. A few things you should be willing to share with your partner and insist upon having shared with you are credit scores and a total disclosure of debt. The seventy-five thousand dollars worth of student loans acquired while obtaining a masters degree in Middle Age Saxon adverbs may have a chilling effect on your passion. Keep your finances separate until you reach a level of commitment requiring you to mingle money. Go in with the full knowledge of what you are taking on, eyes wide open. This is not an area that comes with many pleasant surprises.

Sticker Shock (Factor 11)

Men, when faced with financial wants exceeding their ability to provide, have a poor track record of appropriately handling the situation. Men under this kind of pressure are likely to suffer some degree of depression and often withdraw from fully participating in a relationship. In addition, these men are vulnerable to what Las Vegas calls "gaming" and what Wall Street defines as a "targeted investor." The real name for this kind of behavior is stupidity. Just as we don't intentionally let serial killers operate child care facilities, we shouldn't allow depressed and isolated men to be making financial decisions. Rarely do we see common sense practiced and the outcome is often predictable. If your relationship has "wants" exceeding your "means", don't wait for reality to catch up. If you are single, make sure this model of car is within your means. If you've already bought the Lamborghini, maybe it's a matter of washing and waxing it monthly versus weekly. Have I mentioned the peace of mind a financial plan can provide?

Street Smart (Factor 12)

Two heads are better than one. You need your partner's input when it comes to financial matters. Research has proven men tend to take too many financial risks, while women play it too safe. Not only are the financial decisions likely to be better if both of you are involved, but it also helps to keep a relationship balanced. Ongoing financial education is a must and, in cases where either partner might be financially illiterate, it needs to be a priority. Those who are willing to rely on others to provide and plan for their future are what we can call pets. Keep in mind pets can be neutered at their master's discretion.

Nurture

Even as a man, I can't fully explain why the factors in this segment matter so much. I think part of it has to do with the difference between a relationship and a friendship. While a friendship may provide us with something to eat or someone who listens to us, a relationship seems to add a special value to these actions.

Cooking (Factor 13)

Men aren't exactly after a seven course meal or even a home-cooked meal. While steak and eggs are an excellent way to start the day, having a one pound T-Rex slab from the Bronto Burger delivered for lunch is equally appreciated. For some reason food matters to men, and it tastes even better coming from the woman you love.

Household (Factor 14)

Most animals have a den and men are no different. A man who cannot feel at ease at home will search for a place offering sanctuary. Whether that is the office or a local tavern, a man will go where he can relax. If you're not comfortable at home, what do you need to make this your favored destination? Provided you're happy, make sure you express appreciation and help her to keep it that way.

For our single readers, some special consideration. Your partner's place is what your future home is going to look like someday. Whatever interior decorating dreams you may have, there's not going to be much future employment for you in this department. Instead of concrete flooring get ready for old growth hard wood. The moose head over your bed? Unless the antlers will hold scented candles, expect to find Bullwinkle in the garage. All kidding aside, this is a serious factor. You are looking at a roommate for life and need to make sure things aren't more extreme than you can handle. It's a matter of determining if you are willing to spend the rest of your life weaving through the cat litter boxes or dusting the snow globe collection.

Confidence – single (Factor 15)

Men are naturally reluctant to share. There is a fear that the personal details of our lives will come back around as a very funny story to everyone else but us. In the event what we share isn't funny to our partners, numerous combinations of choice words may be used to describe us. If your partner has the ability to keep a secret and not bring it up while arguing, check to make sure your partner really is female! Essentially, your partner needs to be someone who can be a part of your life in these matters without hurtful consequences.

Dependence – single (Factor 16)

This is a factor that cuts both ways, it just depends on the people in the relationship. We all have differing needs when it comes to personal space. This factor is like sharing a pair of shoes, the closer in foot size you and your partner are, the happier both of you will be. While we all have different personal space requirements, some consideration should be given in certain circumstances. For example, if you have just moved her across the country away from family and friends, her needs may be greater. Unfortunately, this is not one of the more flexible or easily mitigated factors. It pretty much is what it is, plan accordingly.

Harmony- married (Factor 15)

It's always interesting to watch the "recently released" man. In most cases, it's like watching a slow motion tsunami overrun a peaceful village. I attribute the wide swath of destruction that occurs in these men's lives to the "little things." A friend of mine who became divorced learned about the "little things" the hard way. For the first couple of months after the divorce, life was great. The monthly bank statements consisted of a single sheet of paper versus something resembling an IRS tax manual. Reality arrived the morning his power was turned off, his car had been repossessed, and his breakfast consisted of nothing more than ketchup on a saltine cracker.

The "little things" are the foundation of everything. Once the little things are neglected everything begins to crumble. Things like paying bills, buying socks, and taking the dog to the vet may seem insignificant. Small tasks like these have cumulative impacts that you're not going to notice until it's too late. Your best course of action with this factor, regardless of the score, is a steady stream of "thank yous" and finding ways to return the favors as often as possible.

Royalty – married (Factor 16)

Everyone likes to be special, but particularly men. Men strive for recognition and thrive on acknowledgement. It may sound shallow and self-centered, but men really like someone who strokes their ego. Even when it's said like that, men still like it. Personal experience has shown me that if you're not getting at least the "Prince" treatment, it's your own fault. If you are making your partner feel special she is going to have a difficult time restraining herself from returning the favor.

Loyalty

The movies men prefer to watch provide some strong clues as to how men view loyalty. The dialogue in action films may be limited (leaving most of the talking to guns and ammo), but the characters watch each other's back and face their opponents together. That's what it's really about for men, having someone to stand with and watch out for you.

Stand by Your Man (Factor 17)

This may very well be an area where your partner is unaware of her behavior. What may seem like a cute funny story from her point of view may be hurtful to you in the wrong company. If this is the issue, it is important to let your partner know what subjects are private and how some disclosures may impact the intimacy in your relationship.

Your partner also needs to be able to constructively discuss your shortcomings. No one else in your life is going to care enough to take on the negative aspects of your personality, aside from your mother and her view is a bit biased. You have to be mature and open-minded to make this a worthwhile exercise. The truth can hurt and personal growth is rarely pain free: be a man about it! A good starter question may be, "Dear, what is my fatal flaw?", or more honestly, "Dear, what are my fatal flaws?"

Infidelity (Factor 18)

Unless you enjoy the drama that comes with infidelity, neutralizing this factor is the only way to give you peace of mind. Do you have good reason to question your partner's faithfulness? Keep in mind the past is the past; what we really are interested in is the here and now. The objective is to create conditions that will put your mind at ease. Some situations and environments will give you fewer reasons to worry than others. Until a sense of security is established, infidelity fears will stifle your relationship.

Friends (Factors 19, 20)

Friendships are a vital part of a man's mental health. Therefore, it helps to have friends that like your partner. When your friends or partner dislike one another, it may be time to revaluate things. Either your partner has some serious flaws you are blind to or your friends are a bad influence on you. An example might be the monthly "guy's night out." You may need to move the night's ceremonies to your living room or find new friends who require less exotic atmospheres.

Just as your friends need to be evaluated, don't forget your partner's friends. Birds of a feather flock together. Ideally your partner's friends should all belong to the local ladies sewing circle, consisting largely of elderly grandmother types. The problem is you would likely be pressured to attend the men's knitting session held the same night. A person's choice of friends provides an incredible amount of insight into that person's character. Watch the friendship preferences of your partner and yourself very carefully.

BONUS QUESTION
(Factor 21)

This factor has two parts to it. The first part is all about you. Men in general have lousy memories, at least in comparison to women. There are some very good reasons why you may have forgotten her birthday or even what color her eyes are. The problem is you have likely forgotten what those good reasons were as well. Let's face it – you are going to make mistakes that will be very hurtful to your partner. Your responsibility is to own up to these failures and not repeat the same mistakes in the future, or at least not as often. Forgiveness is always a possibility, but forgetting is impossible if you continue to be a repeat offender. If your partner's excellent memory is a result of you repeatedly committing the same crimes, you are the problem.

The second part of this factor is about your partner. What we are identifying here are those women who relish watching their partners make mistakes. A shortcoming is an opportunity for these women to add one more gem to the crown of misery they wear. This behavior is similar to wetting one's pants – there's a warm feeling involved, but is it really the attention anyone should desire? The behavior involved is counterproductive. Your partner gains no real happiness and over time you will lose the desire to change your behavior.

COMMON INTEREST

Think of your relationship like a garden. First you must choose the proper plot of land, then you carefully plan your garden, and finally you sow the seeds with realistic expectations of the site's potential. As the garden grows you must maintain it. If a garden isn't periodically weeded, weeds can take over and consume the nutrients your crop needs. Failure to fertilize and provide adequate water for your garden may not kill it, but the harvest is likely to be disappointing. Not only will you reap what you sow in the end, but there are numerous factors that either increase the yield or contribute to crop failure.

Family & You

The garden-relationship example fits this segment very well. You are not likely to be starting out with a bare plot of earth. There are apt to be trees and flower beds already well established in the garden. While you will have your own plans and varieties you want to plant, the space allotted to you may come with pre-existing conditions. In addition, there may be some species in need of a pruning or requiring the construction of a barrier to keep them out of your space. A firm grasp of the lay of the land will make your efforts much more likely to bear fruit.

In-laws (Factor 22)

There are countless movies where interactions with the in-laws are portrayed as humorous. Unfortunately, real life just isn't that funny and some of you are probably still waiting for a happy ending. If you answered your relationship was "okay" then your in-laws are likely impacting your relationship in a positive way by either supporting the relationship or by not detracting from it. Consider yourself fortunate and be mindful of ways to maintain this relationship. If you answered "poor" then the subject of in-laws can get complicated. A poor relationship with your in-laws not only affects you, but your partner as well. If you think your relationship with your in-laws is difficult, then imagine the position your partner is in. It isn't easy keeping both sides happy.

There may be numerous reasons why your relationship with your in-laws may be less than perfect. These reasons can include personal history, race, religion, education, culture, or simply a clash of personalities. Sometimes these differences can be extremely difficult to resolve. It is important to remember you cannot change your in-laws or how they think; you can only control your own behavior and your reaction to them.

So how do you deal with a poor relationship with your in-laws? There are no easy answers here, as each relationship is unique. Complete avoidance of your in-laws may sound appealing, but is probably unrealistic. Keeping the peace may not always be possible, but you will have better control of the outcome if you and your partner discuss how to handle the conflict beforehand. This at least keeps peace in your relationship and gives you and your partner a united front. Sometimes, a quick "Mom and Dad, your actions are hurting my relationship. If you care about me you will stop doing this," may suffice. Generally, it's not your role to take on your in-laws; it's your partner's job. You can only control your own actions and often the best course of action is simply tolerance.

Future Family Expectations (Factor 23)

Whether you are thinking minivan or a couples Harley, hopefully you and your partner share a similar vision on family planning. Children are one of life's greatest gifts and are often a fundamental part of relationships. That said, children can also be one of life's greatest sources of stress and financial worry. Family planning should not be avoided or ignored. If differences exist, there needs to be a discussion which is open and honest.

We all have personal preferences that should be respected. The emotional, physical, and financial commitments involved with children make this a factor where compromise may not always be possible. If the differences are substantial, your time will be better spent finding a partner with views that parallel your own.

Family – dating with no children under 18 (Factor 24)

Considering the high divorce rate in our society, the odds are (between you and your partner) at least one set of parents will be divorced. Why does this factor matter? Just as communication between two people can be problematic, increasing the number of people involved only further complicates matters. If both sets of parents are still married, you and your partner only have four other people to try to please. If both sets of parents are divorced and have remarried, you and your partner have a potential of eight people to please. Is it really enjoyable trying to split Christmas among four different homes? These outside pressures tend to spill over into your relationship as well. In this case, fewer people equals fewer conflicts, which is never a bad thing for a relationship.

Another underappreciated benefit from having parents that are still married comes in the form of positive role models. Not only can parents provide proof it is possible to stay married, they may even have some insights that can be helpful to your own relationship. While your parents may have separated or failed to provide what could be considered an example of a healthy relationship, that doesn't absolve you from trying. This evaluation should have brought up some ideas as to how your relationship could function more effectively. It's up to you and your partner if someday *your* kids and grandkids will be trying to emulate *your* relationship.

Whether your parents are divorced or married, the reality is parents can cause problems for relationships. You and your partner need to develop a parent plan, ensuring your relationship comes first. Pleasing your parents is somewhere after that.

Family – dating with children under 18 involved (Factor 24)

There is no doubt children are an incredible source of joy in a relationship. However, the problems associated with combining children from past relationships into a new family structure can turn that joy into heartache. Combining families is not to be taken lightly. As the old saying goes, "Blood is thicker than water." As conflicts arise, finding solutions all parties will find satisfactory and equitable can be challenging. The odds are better if only one partner has children under eighteen, but it's still not an easy path. Mixed families can be successful, though they require a lot of hard work, good communication, and additional education. If your relationship fits in this category it would be beneficial to educate yourself. There are well written books and sources on the internet that offer sound advice; you are not the first person with this situation. Be sure to approach this factor with a lot of thought and consideration.

Vacations (*Married, Factor 24*)

A friend of mine once commented, "What is it about kids that suck all the joy out of a woman?" While this is a harsh statement, it does emphasize the importance for couples to spend time alone together without the interruptions of children or other demands. "Couples only" vacations are essential for relationship growth and healing. It is a time to revert to your former self and see your partner as the person you fell in love with. A time absent of emails, business calls, conferences, and other distractions of daily life. The family trip to Grandma's house or the company summer retreat just doesn't count!

Religion
(Factors 25-27)

Religion is a deeply personal factor that everyone experiences in a different way. Wherever strong emotions are mixed with personal preferences, the potential for extreme conflict exists. There are cases where both couples share the same religious beliefs, but have differing levels of spiritual intensity and still find this issue explosive. Religious conflict can be fatal to a relationship due to its sensitive nature. The best option is to avoid a relationship where extreme differences in religious beliefs are involved. The only other option is to develop tolerance and make a point of keeping religion at a distance when it comes to your relationship. The damage that occurs to a relationship trying to settle a religious dispute may be too destructive for the relationship to survive the process or aftermath. Even if your relationship is currently experiencing religious harmony, watch this factor closely. People change as they mature and significant events in life (birth of a child, death of a parent) can bring about sudden shifts in beliefs.

Shared Activities

This is the segment where you learn to fertilize and water your garden. It's not just enough to plant and weed. You have to encourage growth every chance you can. As relationships are a living entity, they are capable of growth and healing when the conditions are right. Optimal growing conditions do not happen by chance, they require the knowledge and skills of a good gardener.

Interests & Activities (Factors 28, 29)

Finding things both you and your partner can enjoy together is important. Part of the fun can be doing new things together as you search for something to share. If you both enjoy something you are more likely to spend time together. The activity or interest isn't nearly as important as the time shared. Just the act of being together allows for other positive experiences to occur. Whether it's small talk, holding hands, or a kiss that leads somewhere – none of these things are a possibility when you are pursuing separate interests.

Beliefs & Values (Factor 30)

When someone reaffirms a belief or view you hold, it generates a positive feeling towards that person. Positive feelings create a connection between you and your partner, further strengthening your bond. Even in cases where you may enjoy a spirited discussion of an issue, it still pays to find areas where you can agree with one another. If agreement is impossible, then you need to develop tolerance which is a process by itself.

Dating (Factor 31)

We usually think of dating as something we do at the start of a relationship. What is the purpose of a date? A date is an opportunity to showcase your best attributes and see what your companion has to offer. Dating can be viewed as a sales job. In the context of a relationship the sales pitch should never end as the product is returnable! Dating provides an opportunity outside of everyday life for couples to remember why they are together and form new memories. It chops, dices, slices, and now it also spices!!! Think sales, do you remember why you brought this product home?

You have now completed the second component of "*Keeping Score*" and are ready for the third component "A Score to Win" starting on page 97.

PART III

A Score to Win

By now you should have a score and a better idea of why the factors influencing this score matter. Now the question becomes what should you do with this score? The table below is a good starting point. This really isn't different from your grade school days, and the grade might become part of your permanent record.

Grade	Score range	What it means
A	90 – 100	Excellent
B	80 – 89	Above average
C	70 – 79	Average
D	60 – 69	Below average
F	59 and below	Failing

I need to make some clear distinctions at this point in time. Single readers have some very different considerations to take into account. If the relationship score is low, it may be time to rethink the relationship and look for another partner. Your selection of a potential life partner may be flawed and the scoring process should have clarified this for you. I once asked a large group of older men what they thought the secret to staying married was. Almost without deviation, they replied, "Marry the right person the first time." Take the relationship evaluation from *Keeping Score* as a reality check. There may be some very good reasons why this relationship shouldn't go any further.

For those readers who are married, this evaluation comes with fewer options. It really is in your best interest to make a good faith effort to work through the problems your relationship may have. Keep in mind the statistics on second and third marriages presented in the beginning of this book; the odds are against you having better luck in the future. I was reminded of this when I got married, by a man who had five failed marriages on his record. His words of advice are unfortunately accurate, "Make the first one work, it's the best chance you'll have." Divorce damages people and like my friend, Tim, you're not going to get out without some scars. In addition, whatever problems you may be dealing with now will have a very good probability of showing up in your future relationships. It should make good sense to fix things now rather than continue repeating the cycle. Today we seem to be better at changing partners than we are at changing what is broken within ourselves.

I need to add a word of caution. If your score is low and your relationship is having problems, be sure to keep things in perspective.

Nearly all the factors making up your score can be improved over time, so don't be too discouraged. As you can now see, relationships are made up of numerous "smaller" things. These smaller things can be changed over time and thus the score can be very different in the future, if you're willing to work at it.

Before you can begin improving your relationship, you have to first change your focus. Up till now the focus has been on how well your partner is performing. The time has come to share scores with your partner and start working on what you can actually influence. This book was never about creating a checklist you could use to humiliate your partner. Rather this book was intended to help you become more of the person your partner needs in his/her life. You can only hope to change another's behavior by first changing your own behavior. The score you have given your partner might happen to be low, there's nothing you can directly do to change that. You can, however, make sure you are holding up your end of things, which may be far more powerful than you realize. One of my daughters was having trouble with some classmates at school. I advised her to smile and be friendly, regardless of what they did or said. A few weeks later I noticed they were all playing together and the bickering had stopped. You have the same choice to make. You can whine all you want about how your partner is shorting you, or you can make sure your partner has no reason to complain about you.

Stop and read the preceding paragraph again. This paragraph is a key part of making relationships work and it runs counter to what we want to do. Our focus tends to be on ourselves and how things are impacting us. It's very natural for us to want our needs and problems to be the focus. Each and every one of us is the star in our own reality show. The reality is – before you can receive you must first give.

So, provided you can make this transition to focusing on the issues you have control over, how do you go about improving a relationship? With your partner, go through all the factors and determine what the status of a factor might be. On the evaluation score sheet there is a slot dedicated to the status of factors. The status of factors can be sorted as follows:

- **Granite** – cannot be changed, it is what it is, will break before it bends

- **Steel** – can be changed over a very long period of time with great effort

- **Plastic** – can be changed over time with moderate effort

- **Tin foil** – easy to change, but can also easily shift shape back to original form

Once you've determined the status of the factors, you can start to prioritize the factors for improvement. Start by looking for factors with the greatest point difference and where you are willing to change. The sections *Common Interest*, *Tried & True*, and *Soul* are good starting points with some of the easier factors to improve upon.

Take things one factor at a time. Some factors will take longer than others to make progress on. The intention should be to change your behavior, not camouflage it. Don't take on too many factors at once or you are likely to be discouraged by the results. Build on success and don't expect immediate improvement. Modifying behavior takes time and a lot of persistence.

How long should it take to go through all the factors and improve your relationship? There's no single answer to this question, as every relationship is different. The score and status of factors will vary greatly depending on the people involved. It's not as important how quickly problems are addressed, but rather that problems stay resolved.

As time goes on, you should find yourself keeping score on *yourself*. Without even thinking about it, you've formed a new habit! In the end that's how lasting change really happens. Another important part of improving your relationship is talking about the factors in this evaluation with your partner. With many of the factors, your partner and you will have different thoughts and life experiences influencing your choices. Work together as a couple to identify these differences and understand how they affect one another. Because your relationship involves two people, a relationship can only be as happy as the lowest score.

A quick review of the key points if *Keeping Score* is going to work for your relationship:

- The score is only a starting point, not the ending value of a relationship. To change something you must first measure it. What you will not measure you cannot manage or influence. The attention needs to be on improving the "little things." In time the score will reflect your efforts.

- Focus first on modifying your own behavior, even if it means taking the first step. A mentor of mine once told me, "Nine times out of ten, if you try, you will succeed. The biggest problem is most people will never even try." This advice holds especially true for relationships. Don't be the one waiting for an apology or for your partner to change. Take the first step and try.

- Be patient, creating something of lasting value takes time and relationships can last a lifetime. Be persistent, success is only found before work in the dictionary. Those who can celebrate one year, twenty years, or fifty years of marriage have made it there one day at a time.

It's a given this book would have an ending. What about your relationship? Have you and your partner learned anything? While this book has an ending, let's hope this is just the beginning for your relationship. Writing this book has been a source of great insight into my own relationship and the experience has been rewarding. We all have a stake in seeing relationships flourish. Better relationships mean functional families, stronger communities, and a more prosperous nation.

In order to further test the principles of this book and to comment, please visit the website **www.keepingscorebook.com**. In addition, you can enter your scores and compare your relationship to others. Thank you for taking the time to read this book, I hope it helps. Best of luck to you and your partner; may your journey be a rewarding one.

Score Key – Eve

Factor	a	b	c	d	e
Big Sword vs Broken Sword					
Castle or Cave					
1	7	4			
2	8	4	0		
King or Squire					
3	0	2	3	4	5
4	5	4	3	1	0
5	5	3	2	0	
Income Balance					
6	3	2	1		
7	4	0			
8	4	0			
9	4	0			

	a	b	c	d	e
Tried & True					
Handle with Care					
10	0	1	2	3	
11	2	0			
12	3	2	1	0	
13	2	1	0		
Tango Time					
14	3	2	0		
15	2	0			
16	0	2			
17	3	2	0		
Make the Heart Race					
18	1	0			
19	2	1	0		
20	2	1	0		
21	3	0			
22	2	0			

Score Key – Eve

Factor	a	b	c
Bonus			
23	10	5	0

Common Interest		
Family & You		
24	1	0
25	2	0
26	0	1	2
Religion		
27	2	0
28	2	0
29	1	0
Shared Activities		
30	1	0
31	1	0
32	1	0
33	2	0

Score Key – Adam

Factor	a	b	c	d
Wonder Woman				
The Goods				
1	5	4	3	1
2	5	4	3	1
3	5	4	3	1
Hair				
4	5	4	3	1
5	5	4	3	1
6	5	4	3	1
Armor				
7	5	4	3	0
8	5	4	3	0
9	5	4	3	0

Soul				
Financial				
10	0	4	2	
11	3	0	1	
12	3	2	0	
Nurture				
13	0	1	2	
14	2	1	0	
15	3	2	0	
16	3	2	1	0
Loyalty				
17	3	2	0	
18	0	1	3	
19	2	1		
20	2	1	0	

Score Key – Adam

Factor	a	b	c
Bonus			
21	0	5	10

Common Interest		
Family & You		
22	1	0	
23	2	0	
24	0	1	2
Religion		
25	2	0	
26	2	0	
27	1	0	
Shared Activities		
28	1	0	
29	1	0	
30	1	0	
31	2	0	

How to Fill Out the Evaluation Sheets

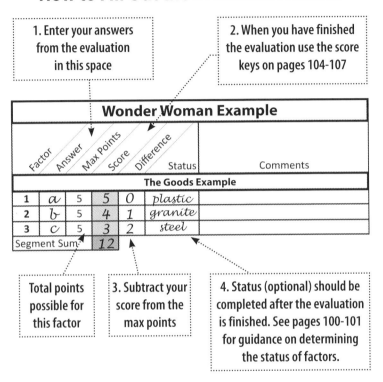

1. Enter your answers from the evaluation in this space

2. When you have finished the evaluation use the score keys on pages 104-107

Wonder Woman Example

Factor	Answer	Max Points	Score	Difference	Status	Comments
The Goods Example						
1	a	5	5	0	plastic	
2	b	5	4	1	granite	
3	c	5	3	2	steel	
Segment Sum			12			

Total points possible for this factor

3. Subtract your score from the max points

4. Status (optional) should be completed after the evaluation is finished. See pages 100-101 for guidance on determining the status of factors.

Evaluation Sheets – Eve

Big Sword vs Broken Sword

Factor	Answer	Max Points	Score	Difference	Status	Comments
Castle or Cave						
1		7				
2		8				
Segment Sum						

King or Squire

Factor	Answer	Max Points	Score	Difference	Status	Comments
3		5				
4		5				
5		5				
Segment Sum						

Income Balance

Factor	Answer	Max Points	Score	Difference	Status	Comments
6		3				
7		4				
8		4				
9		4				
Segment Sum						

Evaluation Sheets – Eve

Tried & True

Factor	Answer	Max Points	Score	Difference	Status	Comments
Handle with Care						
10		3				
11		2				
12		3				
13		2				
Segment Sum						

Tango Time						
14		3				
15		2				
16		2				
17		3				
Segment Sum						

Make the Heart Race						
18		1				
19		2				
20		2				
21		3				
22		2				
Segment Sum						

Bonus						
23		10				

Evaluation Sheets – Eve

Common Interest						
Factor	Answer	Max Points	Score	Difference	Status	Comments
Family & You						
24		1				
25		2				
26		2				
Segment Sum						

Religion						
27		2				
28		2				
29		1				
Segment Sum						

Shared Activities						
30		1				
31		1				
32		1				
33		2				
Segment Sum						

Evaluation Sheets – Eve

Big Sword vs Broken Sword	Max Points	Score	Difference
Castle or Cave	15		
King or Squire	15		
Income Balance	15		
Section Sum			

Tried & True	Max Points	Score	Difference
Handle with Care	10		
Tango Time	10		
Make the Heart Race	10		
Section Sum			

Bonus	Max Points	Score	Difference
Bonus	10		
Section Sum			

Common Interest	Max Points	Score	Difference
Family & You	5		
Religion	5		
Shared Activities	5		
Section Sum			

Keeping Score	Max Points	Score	Difference
Big Sword vs Broken Sword	45		
Tried & True	30		
Bonus	10		
Common Interest	15		
Sum of Sections	100		

Evaluation Sheets – Adam

Wonder Woman

Factor	Answer	Max Points	Score	Difference	Status	Comments
The Goods						
1		5				
2		5				
3		5				
Segment Sum						

Hair						
4		5				
5		5				
6		5				
Segment Sum						

Armor						
7		5				
8		5				
9		5				
Segment Sum						

Evaluation Sheets – Adam

Soul						
Factor	Answer	Max Points	Score	Difference	Status	Comments
Financial						
10		4				
11		3				
12		3				
Segment Sum						

Nurture						
13		2				
14		2				
15		3				
16		3				
Segment Sum						

Loyalty						
17		3				
18		3				
19		2				
20		2				
Segment Sum						

Bonus						
21		10				

Evaluation Sheets – Adam

Common Interest

Factor	Answer	Max Points	Score	Difference	Status	Comments
Family & You						
22	1					
23	2					
24	2					
Segment Sum						

Religion						
25	2					
26	2					
27	1					
Segment Sum						

Shared Activities						
28	1					
29	1					
30	1					
31	2					
Segment Sum						

Evaluation Sheets – Adam

Wonder Woman	Max Points	Score	Difference
The Goods	15		
Hair	15		
Armor	15		
Section Sum			

Soul	Max Points	Score	Difference
Financial	10		
Nurture	10		
Loyalty	10		
Section Sum			

Bonus	Max Points	Score	Difference
Bonus	10		
Section Sum			

Common Interest	Max Points	Score	Difference
Family & You	5		
Religion	5		
Shared Activities	5		
Section Sum			

Keeping Score	Max Points	Score	Difference
Wonder Woman	45		
Soul	30		
Bonus	10		
Common Interest	15		
Sum of Sections	100		